BIRDS FLY OUT BEHIND THE SUN
AND WITH THEM I'LL BE LEAVING.

FROM 'OCTOBER SONG'
ROBIN WILLIAMSON

Printed in Shenzhen, China

Publisher's Cataloging-in-Publication Data:

Ross, Warren, 1953-
Red boots and assorted things /
Warren Ross[and] Victoria Usova.
pages cm
ISBN: 978-0-9903086-2-1 (hardcover)
1. Watercolor painting. 2. Wit and humor.
3. Imagination—Fiction. 4. Picture books.
I. Usova, Victoria.II. Title.
PS439 .U86 2016
817`.6—dc23

RED BOOTS
AND
ASSORTED THINGS

ART BY VICTORIA USOVA

TEXT BY WARREN ROSS

A long time ago,
we had a home in the sky.

Gravity is fun.
It works every time.

Tamarind asked the poppies
to ask the pears
to ask the cat
to please bring the tea.

Drucilla's new town was different.

I have a dollar fifty-nine to spend.
I'm buying Onion Rides for all my friends.

The little fish
asked the big fish
if she was tired
of swimming around
with a village on her back.

Through that green door
I knew what never was.
I knew some things
I can't remember now.
Those things are real, I know —
I don't know how.

The cat had hoped for Chopin.

I like Dwight. He's big and white.
He roams around the roofs at night.
He doesn't bump or kick or bite.
Go up and see. He's quite a sight.

When the wind blows,
things come and go.
Wind is a thing too.
It comes and goes
and flies and flows
and flaps your muffler in your face.

Let's go here.
No, let's go there.
No, let's go everywhere.
Well anyway, we can't go now,
unless you let me bring along my cow.

The flying horses
neigh and dance and play.
I hope they stay.

But if they go, my Mom will say
tomorrow is another day
and more good things
will come our way.